JACQUES
CARTIER

KEN ROBERTS

CANADIAN PATHFINDERS SERIES

Grolier Limited
TORONTO

Cover illustration: Colin Gillies

Illustrations: Penelope Moir, pages 11, 19

Photo credits: Public Archives of Canada, pages 4 (C-11226), 7 (C-3686), 14 (C-8274), 21 (C-5933), 23 (C-42247), 25 (C-10489), 27 (C-8028), 28 (C-120163), 30 (C-12235), 33 (C-5538), 36 (C-41570) 40 (C-120161), 41 (C-113345), 45 (C-24150); National Map Collection, pages 8 (NMC-21090), 42-43 (NMC-40461); Metropolitan Toronto Library Board, page 12; Musée du Québec, page 16 (ACMQ-77-156; photo by Patrick Altman); Confederation Life Collection, page 18 (52-267-19); Hudson's Bay Company Archives, page 35 (P-374); Environment Canada, Parks, page 38.

Canadian Cataloguing in Publication Data

Roberts, Ken, 1946–
    Jacques Cartier

(Canadian pathfinders series)
For use in schools.
Includes index.
ISBN 0-7172-2507-0

1. Cartier, Jacques, 1491–1557—Juvenile literature.
2. America—Discovery and exploration—French—Juvenile literature.
3. Explorers—Canada—Biography—Juvenile literature.
4. Explorers—France—Biography—Juvenile literature.
I. Title.   II. Series.

FC301.C37R62 1988   971.01'13'0924   C88-094616-4
E133.C3R62 1988

123456789   ML   7654321098

Printed and Bound in Canada.

Contents

4

Prologue

On a beautiful fall afternoon, sixteen hundred kilometres from the open sea, Jacques Cartier stood on a hilltop above the St. Lawrence River.

Cartier was excited. He looked to the north and saw an endless, rolling forest. Someplace out there, according to his native guides, stood the Kingdom of Saguenay, a rich land whose gold could help make Cartier's greedy King rich.

To the west Cartier saw the St. Lawrence narrow into rapids. He named the rapids Lachine, the "China" rapids. He had heard of a huge sea beyond the river. Surely, he thought, he had found the much searched for seaway to the Far East.

Cartier turned to walk back down the hill. By the north shore stood a huge native stockade surrounded by cultivated fields.

Jacques Cartier had travelled farther into the vast New World than any other explorer. He had seen a lush, rich land and written of its staggering beauty. As Jacques Cartier walked down the hill he made plans to come back to this place, to sail beyond the rapids and to find the Kingdom of Saguenay.

But Cartier's nightly diary would soon lose its sense of wonder. Instead, it would tell of his fear for survival. The winter would be far colder and longer than he had ever imagined, and the Iroquois would not always be so friendly. Jacques Cartier, the gifted sailor and map maker, would soon be asked to use different skills.

Jacques Cartier would survive. But he would never sail past the rapids nor search the hills for Saguenay.

The Early Years

Jacques Cartier was born in the small French fishing port of St. Malo in 1491, the year before Columbus made his first voyage to the New World.

When Jacques was six years old the English explorer John Cabot sailed along the coast of Newfoundland and wrote in his diary that fish were so plentiful "they sometimes stopped the progress of the ships."

News of Cabot's remarkable discovery quickly spread. In St. Malo, as elsewhere, the fishermen had always fished close to land. Now, some of them decided to cross the treacherous Atlantic and fill their nets.

The fishing boats of St. Malo sailed together the following spring along the shore of Scotland and then across the ocean to Newfoundland. It was a dangerous journey, and some of the ships sank. But the fishing grounds were as rich as John Cabot had promised. The trip to the New World became an annual event for the fishermen of St. Malo. As a teenager Cartier joined the fishing fleet and sailed to the Grand Banks. He probably made the trip a number of times.

Few fishermen were interested in exploration or in writing of what they saw. They wanted to fill their boats with cod and leave the New World quickly, getting their cargoes to market while the fish were still edible. (Their fish were salted for the long journey home.)

Most of the St. Malo sailors knew little about navigation. They sailed for the New World in convoys, hoping they would not become lost. Their boats carried only a primitive compass to help them

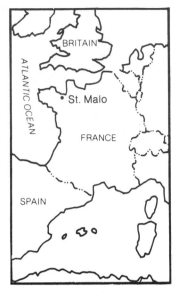

Jacques Cartier was born in St. Malo in France.

How the cod were processed. The fish were gutted then split open, salted, and laid on racks in the sun to dry.

navigate. The compass usually consisted of a long piece of magnetized metal, hung by a piece of rope. Such compasses were impossible to use when seas were rough.

Cartier was more interested in navigation than he was in fishing. He soon became expert at charting currents and reading a compass.

In 1519, when Cartier was twenty-eight years old, he married Catherine Des Granches, the

Giovanni Verrazzano

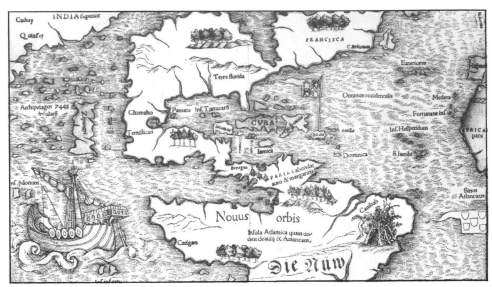

Sebastien Münster produced this woodcut map in 1540, after Cartier's visit to North America. It reflects Verrazzano's exploration of the Atlantic coast between North Carolina and New York. Its vague and inaccurate depiction of Canada indicates that Münster was unaware of Cartier's explorations.

The French were late entrants in the race to explore and claim land in the New World. Giovanni Verrazzano, an Italian navigator, was the first explorer sent west as an official representative of France. His job, like Cartier's later, was to search both for gold and a route to China.

Verrazzano set off on his first voyage in 1524 with four ships. Two were lost in a storm before leaving the English Channel. The others sailed along the coast of Spain and captured a Spanish ship filled with gold. One of Verrazzano's ships took the gold back to France while the other sailed for the New World. Verrazzano arrived near North Carolina and sailed up the coast, discovering the harbour at present-day New York City. He found no gold or route to the Far East.

Verrazzano's second voyage for the French took him to Brazil.

According to some sources, on a third voyage, Verrazzano was caught by the Spanish and hanged as a pirate.

daughter of a town official in St. Malo. Cartier is listed on the marriage certificate as being a "master pilot" or navigator.

Cartier served as a navigator for coastal trading vessels and fishing convoys to the New World for many years, but he wanted to chart new waters. Although there are few clues to Cartier's life before becoming an explorer, he probably travelled with the explorer Giovanni Verrazzano on a trip to Brazil in 1528. In his journals Cartier later compared plants in Canada with those in Brazil and shortly after the end of Verrazzano's voyage, Cartier's wife, Catherine, acted as godmother for a woman identified only as "Catharine du Brezil."

It was common practice for explorers to return from the New World bringing a few of the native people with them. They were taught European languages so that they might act as interpreters on future voyages.

In 1533 the King of France, Francis I, decided to send an expedition to the New World. King Francis was almost broke. Lavish parties and a lengthy war with the Holy Roman emperor, Charles V, kept him scrounging for money. He hoped to find riches in the New World.

The Spanish and the Portuguese had already divided and claimed most of South and Central America, and Francis knew he could not compete with them. Instead, he wanted to explore the northern part of the New World. The King's High Admiral suggested the expedition be led by Jacques Cartier.

Cartier was called before the King and interviewed at the coastal castle of Mont St. Michel, a fairytale castle built on a high rock off the beach. Francis was impressed with Cartier and granted him permission to find and outfit two ships. Sixty-one men including Cartier were to make the journey.

Cartier was excited, but when he returned to St. Malo the fishermen there wanted nothing to do with his ridiculous voyage. Fishing offered them a more secure income and many worried about risking their lives. Other fishermen opposed the whole idea of exploration. If better maps were available, they argued, other fisherman might decide to make the journey and New World fish would sell for a cheaper price.

In March, 1534, the court at St. Malo issued a proclamation stating that no fishing vessels could leave St. Malo until Cartier had his full crew. There was a lot of grumbling, but the threat worked. Cartier was ready to sail by the middle of April.

The morning of April 20, 1534, was sunny but cool. Cartier's crew assembled on the dock. One by one the Vice Admiral of France made them take an oath of allegiance to the King and to their commander, Jacques Cartier. The sailors said their final good-byes to family and friends and boarded the two small ships. Then, just as many fishermen had done in the past, Cartier and his crew set sail for the New World.

The three voyages of Jacques Cartier would result neither in treasures of gold nor a trade route to China. They would not offer much help to a troubled King Francis I.

They were instead to have a far greater effect on the land towards which he sailed.

The First Voyage

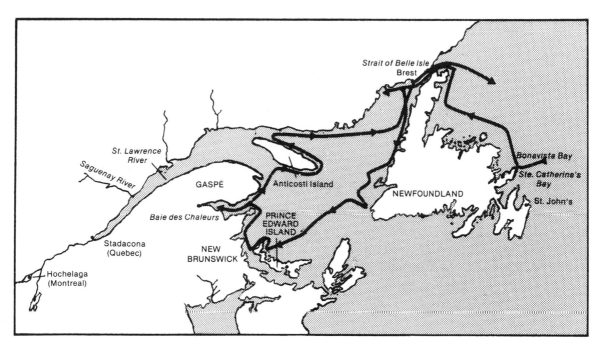

Cartier's first voyage.

Cartier made the Atlantic crossing in only twenty days, arriving exactly where he had meant to—Bonavista Bay on the east coast of Newfoundland.

The harbour, however, was still blocked with winter ice and Cartier's two ships could not enter. Sailing south, Cartier found another bay and named it Ste. Catherine's, after his wife. Here, the two small ships were pulled up onto the beach and overhauled. Cartier wanted to make sure his ships were in good condition before they continued the voyage.

Cartier had a plan. The small strait dividing Newfoundland and Labrador at the top is the strait of Belle Isle and is famous for strong currents and rough waters. Cartier thought that the current in the strait was too strong to be caused only by the ocean

11

Francis I
King of France

Francis I became King in 1515 when he was twenty years old. He was a charming, clever man with an enormous love for parties.

It was Francis' great misfortune to be King of France during the time Charles V was Holy Roman Emperor. The Holy Roman Empire was made up of Spain, the Netherlands, and much of Germany. It was Charles' ambition to include France in this vast political state. As a result, he and Francis were constantly at war.

Francis became interested in the New World when Cortés, fighting under the banner of Charles V, found massive treasures in Mexico. After the discovery of Inca gold Francis funded Cartier's first voyage. He needed money desperately. At that time he had been taken prisoner by Charles and released when he promised to pay 2,000,000 gold crowns as ransom.

Francis I hoped that Cartier's voyages would result in an instant cure for his financial problems.

pushing itself through the small opening. He thought some other large body of water must be affecting the waters of the Strait, and he planned to follow the current. This would, he hoped, lead him to a river or channel which cut across the continent.

For several weeks Cartier's two small ships were unable to sail through the Strait of Belle Isle because storms and rough waters kept stopping them. They finally sailed through on June 9. Near Brest, Labrador, Cartier reported seeing European fishermen, and he actually helped one vessel which had lost its way.

Cartier was not impressed with the barren Labrador countryside. He wrote in his diary: "I did not see a cartload of good earth."

The ships continued to sail south. Cartier made many detailed maps of the western coast of Newfoundland as they went, giving names to many bays and rivers. Some of these names remain today.

Europeans at the time did not realize Newfoundland was an island, since they used only the northern passage. Cartier did not sail far enough to discover the truth. Instead, he followed a mysterious current towards the Gulf of St. Lawrence.

The islands to the west of Newfoundland were as pleasant and beautiful as Labrador had been harsh: "One acre of this land is worth more than all the New Land," Cartier wrote.

Cartier explored and charted Prince Edward Island and much of the coast of New Brunswick. His journal is filled with praise for the beauty of the landscape, concluding that the land was "hotter than Spain and the most beautiful a man could see."

As a navigator, Cartier knew he was only slightly north of Paris, and he assumed the winters would be mild. For a while, he considered spending the coming winter, even though he had not brought extra supplies. He assumed the land could supply plenty of food and that no extra clothes would be necessary.

One July day, in the Baie des Chaleurs, Cartier was in a longboat, charting the coastline when his men spotted a fleet of canoes racing towards them.

Cartier on his travels.

14

Cartier and his men frantically began to row back to their ships but the canoeists were faster and Cartier and his men found themselves surrounded. He was ready for such an emergency. Each of his ships was equipped with four small cannon, little use in a fight but capable of making a great deal of noise. Cartier signalled his ships and two of the cannon were fired. The canoes turned away and Cartier's crew rowed back to their ships.

The canoeists returned in about an hour and circled the two French ships cautiously. Cartier ordered his men to fire a musket volley over the heads of the people in the canoes and they scattered once again. After realizing no harm had been done, they came back a third time. Cartier ordered his men to put down their muskets and hand out small gifts. The two sides began to trade.

Cartier is the first known European to trade for North American furs. He did not, however, realize how important furs were to become in the development of Canada and in his journals twice called them "a thing of little value."

A few days later, in the Gaspé basin, Cartier met another group of native people. They were the Huron-Iroquois, who normally lived along the St. Lawrence River but came to the coast during the summer to fish.

On July 25, Cartier and most of his men rowed to shore and cut down several large trees. With the Iroquois watching, the French sailors lashed several tree trunks together to make a huge ten metre tall cross. In large letters across the beam they carved the words "VIVE LE ROI DE FRANCE". Cartier's

The Arrival of
Jacques Cartier,
*painted by
John David
Kelley.*

crew then carried the heavy cross to the beach, dug a hole, and stood it upright. While the Iroquois watched, Cartier conducted a solemn ceremony. Cartier and his men then returned to their ships.

The Iroquois did not like these men from the sea erecting anything on their land. They raced to the French ships in their canoes. Their chief, Donnacona, stood up in his canoe and, according to Cartier, angrily "pointed to the land all around us, as if to say that all the land was his, and that we should not have planted the cross without permission."

The Iroquois circled Cartier's ships. Cartier's crew stood with their muskets ready and cannon aimed. But Cartier did not want to fight. He knew he would need help to explore farther.

Cartier held out an axe to Donnacona as if he were offering it as a gift. Donnacona's canoe slowly circled closer and closer, until it was right beside the French vessel. Donnacona reached up for the axe. Quickly, Cartier's men caught hold of the canoe and pulled it close to their ship. They pulled Donnacona and two of his grown sons on board.

Cartier tried to calm the angry chief, offering gifts. Using sign language, Cartier tried to explain that he wanted to take the two young men with him, promising to bring them back. Donnacona had little choice but to agree.

Cartier wanted the two Iroquois to help him discover more about this rich new land and to teach them French so they could act as interpreters. He would keep his promise to Donnacona, but the old chief was not to see his sons for one whole year.

Cartier sailed to Anticosti Island. He again

considered spending the winter in Canada but was
persuaded by his crew to sail back home. Not
knowing about the southern route around
Newfoundland, the ships sailed through the Strait of
Belle Isle and arrived back at St. Malo on September
5, 1534.

*Cartier meets with
native people on the
Gaspé shore near
Percé Rock.*

The Second Voyage Begins

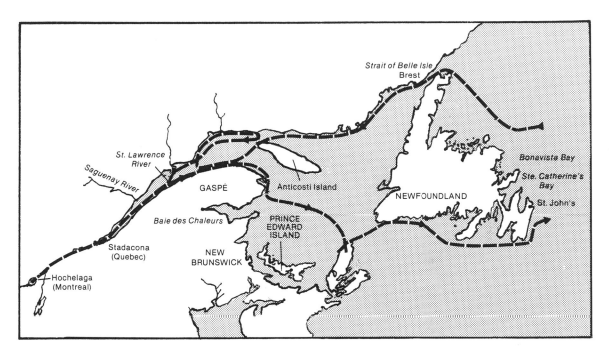

Cartier's second voyage.

Cartier had discovered neither gold nor a passage to China. Still, he did have evidence that both were waiting to be found. The two young Iroquois, Domagaya and Taignoagny, were learning French. They told of a great river and of a kingdom named Saguenay, rich with copper and gold.

King Francis I believed them, and he commissioned a new expedition. Cartier's glowing descriptions of the lands below Labrador, together with King Francis' enthusiasm, attracted some "gentlemen of rank" to join Cartier. This time no threat was needed to recruit a crew. There were ample volunteers.

On May 19, 1535, Jacques Cartier left St. Malo in command of the *Grande Hermine* and two smaller vessels, the *Petite Hermine* and the *Emerillon*. He had supplies for fifteen months. Domagaya and Taignoagny sailed with Cartier on the *Grande Hermine*.

Cartier thought the two natives were now loyal to him and that they would stay with him even after seeing their village again. This wasn't true. Taignoagny and Domagaya were anxious to return to their people. The long Atlantic crossing may have strengthened their decision to leave Cartier.

It was a hard voyage. Cartier's ship reached the eastern shore of Newfoundland on July 7, but the two smaller vessels did not arrive until July 26. It was already midsummer, a time when many fishing vessels were beginning to leave.

Cartier's small fleet sailed through the Strait of Belle Isle, towards the gulf. He found one bay, "full of islands and good entrances," which he called St. Laurent (St. Lawrence). Soon the name would be given to the gulf and the great river beyond it. But there were so many islands and peninsulas that Cartier could not yet find the path which led to the broad river.

Domagaya and Taignoagny were anxious to reach their home. They knew the area well and decided to help Cartier. On August 13, 1535, they told him that Anticosti was not a peninsula, as he had thought, but an island. On the far side, they said, began the Kingdom of Saguenay and beyond Saguenay was Canada. Cartier's journal entry on this day is the first mention we have of the name *Canada*. He does not say what the word might have meant.

Cartier sailed around the island and into the St.

Lawrence River. Word of the large ships travelled fast, and the villages along each shore were crowded with people. Canoes accompanied Cartier's ships as they travelled.

Almost a hundred years after Cartier's voyage up the St. Lawrence a native from Quebec told a French priest a story his grandmother told, of giant moving islands which carried strange men who ate wood (hard ship's biscuits) and drank blood (red wine).

Cartier's three ships.

On September 7, 1535, Cartier arrived at a group of islands his two Iroquois interpreters said was "the beginning of the land and province of Canada." They were more than twelve hundred kilometres from the ocean, near where Quebec City stands today. The three ships dropped anchor and a party of men rowed out to a beautiful island, where wild grapes grew in abundance. Cartier first called the island Bacchus but later changed its name to Ile d'Orléans. Domagaya and Taignoagny had come home.

The Iroquois village, Stadacona, was perched high on the bluffs of the northern shore. The day after Cartier arrived Donnacona, "Lord of Canada," came to see him. The two men exchanged gifts.

Domagaya and Taignoagny returned to their village and began to work against the French. Taignoagny pointed out that Cartier's men always carried guns to friendly meetings but did not like the Iroquois to be armed. Taignoagny also suggested the French could pay far more for furs and food and help.

Cartier found a spot where the Sainte-Croix River (now the St-Charles) flowed into the St. Lawrence to pull his ships onto shore and create a camp. He kept the Sainte-Croix River between his camp and the large Iroquois village.

Cartier told Donnacona he wanted to explore westward on the St. Lawrence and needed guides. Donnacona objected. There was nothing to see, he said, using Taignoagny as an interpreter. Cartier insisted. There would be no help, warned Donnacona. Cartier said he would go without guides.

Taignoagny did not want Cartier to trade

*Cartier reaches the
village of Hochelaga.*

directly with the villages upriver. He wanted
Stadacona to become a trading centre so his people
would benefit.

A few days later a canoe floated past Cartier's
ships. Inside were three Iroquois, who acted out a
noisy chant and then bent over as if dead.
Taignoagny interpreted the dance, telling Cartier that
it was a message from the god Cudouagny warning
the French they would not live through the winter if
they tried to travel any farther.

The threat did not work. Cartier and fifty men

set sail in the *Emerillon* and headed west. The scenery they passed was magnificent. They saw huge golden and red forests that Cartier said contained the "finest trees in the world." Near Richelieu Rapids Cartier left twenty men and the *Emerillon* at a large Iroquois camp and continued upriver in a longboat.

After thirteen days, Cartier and his men arrived at the site of what is now Montreal. Here they found a huge Iroquois village called Hochelaga, the most impressive community Cartier would see in the New World. The village was surrounded by a triple stockade of sharpened logs, with platforms on which rested stacks of rocks that could be used to repel invaders.

Cartier and some of his men, along with hundreds of Iroquois, climbed the tall hill just behind Hochelaga and named it Mount Royal, in honour of King Francis. From the top Cartier looked to the west and saw rapids in the river. Using sign language, his native guides told him that, once past the rapids, it was possible to canoe upstream for more than three months and in many places there was so much water that the horizon could not be seen.

Cartier named the rapids Lachine, the China rapids. He thought he had found the missing gateway to the Orient.

Looking northward, Cartier saw beautiful, fall-coloured hills. His guides pointed to metal objects held by the French and then pointed north. Cartier took this to mean the Kingdom of Saguenay lay still farther ahead.

Jacques Cartier stayed in Hochelaga for only one day. Then, he and his men returned to the *Emerillon* and sailed back down the St. Lawrence, ready to spend the winter in this vast, beautiful land. Cartier's job was to find a path through the continent, but he was beginning to realize that the New World itself was filled with promise.

An old woodcut showing the layout and the surroundings of Hochelaga.

When Taignoagny had warned Cartier not to travel upriver he said the Iroquois god Cudouagny would send so much snow and ice the French would all perish. The prediction would almost come true. Many Frenchmen would not survive the winter ahead.

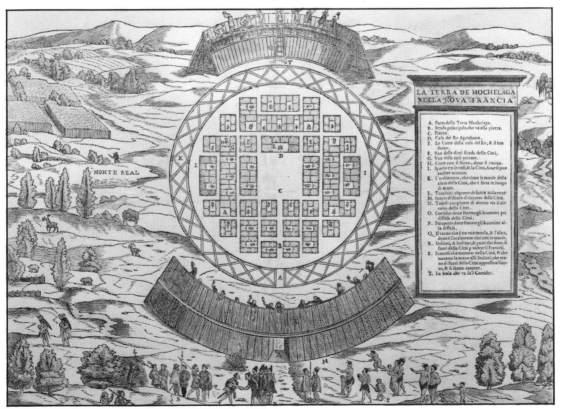

Winter in Canada

While Cartier was gone, the natives at Stadacona had become even more hostile. Cartier was surprised, when he sailed up in the *Emerillon,* to discover his men had built a stockade around the beached ships. The ships were, wrote Cartier, "completely enclosed by heavy timbers planted upright and joined one to another, and armed with artillery all around." A fort, then, became the first structure built by Europeans away from the coast of Canada.

Cartier ordered his men to dig a moat around the stockade, diverting part of the Sainte-Croix River so that the ditch would fill with water. Using rope and pulleys from ship's rigging, his men also constructed a drawbridge at the entrance to the stockade. Cartier ordered that fifty men stay on duty at all times, marching, playing bugles, hammering, and doing whatever seemed necessary to convince the watchful Iroquois that they were always prepared for an assault.

Cartier managed to negotiate a weak peace with Donnacona before the snows began to fall. Cartier's crew and the natives feasted together one last time, but trading stopped.

In mid-November the Sainte-Croix River froze. The moat, dug with such effort and care, disappeared under mounds of snow. Cartier could not believe so much snow could fall on one place. He liked to take walks around the fort, usually with an escort, but often found himself stuck inside the stockade.

When off duty, Cartier's men remained on board the ships. The vessels made terrible winter living quarters. European sailing ships were made for the open sea, not for ice and cold. There were no

None of the existing portraits of Cartier is known to be authentic. This nineteenth-century engraving is one representation of what he might have looked like.

fireplaces. Sailors were reluctant to light fires on their wooden vessels. There was no insulation either. During the winter the ice on the inside of the living quarters was more than four fingers thick. Snow often drifted higher than the sides of the ships. The main source of heat was the warmth given off by each person in the cramped living quarters.

Freezing temperatures proved a minor problem compared with disease. Cartier and his crew relied on cured meats and stale bread to get them through the winter. They could not hunt because they had neither snowshoes nor traps. They did not trade for fresh food because they did not know it would be better for

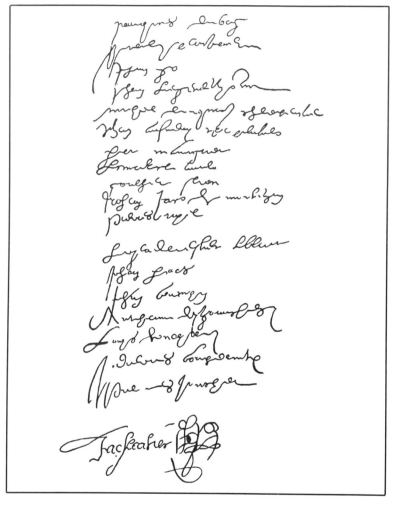

The last page of the list of Cartier's crew for his second voyage. Cartier's signature appears at the bottom.

them and that the vitamins from fresh food were necessary to prevent the disease scurvy.

Scurvy is a painful illness which weakens tissue and damages internal organs. Before the end of the year eight sailors were dead and only a handful were healthy. Cartier was one of the healthy ones, partly because fresh food was always given to the captain. Eventually, almost the entire crew suffered from scurvy, and no one who had contracted the disease recovered. Surely, thought Cartier, the Iroquois would attack when they discovered how weak the French had become. Even if a few men should survive the winter cold, scurvy, and an Iroquois attack, there would not be enough of them to sail even one ship back to the fishing grounds.

Cartier did not give up. He ordered anyone healthy enough to swing an arm to smack the sides of the ships when the Iroquois were near.

Despite these efforts Cartier knew he was merely marking time. By the end of February, twenty-five men had died.

One day, to his surprise, Cartier met Domagaya by the river bank. Ten days earlier Cartier had noticed signs of scurvy around Domagaya's face. Now, Domagaya was healthy and smiling. All signs of the illness had vanished.

Cartier realized that there was a cure for scurvy and the Iroquois knew it! Cartier made up a story. He told Domagaya that a servant, whom Domagaya liked, had been stricken with scurvy. Calmly, he asked how Domagaya had been cured. Domagaya shrugged and called two women, telling them to show Cartier the cure. The women led Cartier to a white cedar tree and explained that the bark and leaves, when boiled, made a "tea" which cured the disease.

Cartier rushed back to his stockade with some of the leaves. Sick as they were, many of the ailing sailors distrusted the foul smelling drink he made, knowing it came from the hostile Iroquois. One sailor

Scurvy

Cartier is shown what is needed to cure scurvy.

Scurvy is caused by a lack of vitamin C. Wounds heal slowly and tissues eventually become thin and weak. It is difficult for stitches to hold in scurvy stricken skin. As scurvy advances the gums become sore, teeth fall out, joints stiffen, and the victim dies in great pain. Someone suffering from scurvy can be completely cured if vitamin C is reintroduced into the diet.

Sixteenth-century sailors carried foods which could not be ruined by exposure to dampness on long voyages. Unfortunately, these foods were low in vitamin C. The age of exploration meant longer voyages and incredibly high death rates due to scurvy.

The problem was not solved quickly. It was not until 1795 that the British navy became the first to issue, officially, citrus juice to its sailors. British sailors became known as "Limeys" since the lime was the most frequently used source of vitamin C.

decided to try it anyway. His mates, lying in hammocks, watched as he sipped the tea.

Nothing happened. The brave sailor drank the rest and then had some more before going to sleep. The next morning, when the sailor woke up, he asked for still more. He was already beginning to recover. His shipmates cheered and sent their healthy comrades out to chop down one whole cedar tree and bring it back to the fort.

In a few short weeks, all signs of the disease had vanished and the entire crew had completely recovered. It was a "true and manifest miracle," wrote Cartier with relief.

Realizing the Iroquois could teach him a great deal about how to survive in the forests of Canada, Cartier began to observe Donnacona and his tribe more closely. He filled his journal with information about such things as Iroquois marriage customs and sense of communal ownership. In the spring he wrote detailed accounts of crops and native methods of curing meat. He wrote about tobacco and the native habit of smoking it in pipes. Cartier even took a puff and wrote that his mouth "seemed filled with flaming hot pepper."

Cartier's problems were not over, though. Domagaya and Taignoagny had left Stadacona to visit other tribes along the river. They spoke out against the French and told of the riches in their three small ships. Cartier, watching the village as he did, noticed that more and more warriors were beginning to gather. He knew an attack was being planned, and he knew that his guns and cannon, for all their noise, were a pitiful protection.

The Return Home

Quietly, Cartier prepared his ships for sailing and
made his plans. He was in a difficult situation. He
was twelve hundred kilometres from the open sea
with many hostile villages to pass. Besides, his ships
were not designed for fighting, particularly on a river.

Cartier needed some way of stopping the
Iroquois from attacking. He decided to kidnap
Donnacona, chief of all the land then called Canada.
There could be no native attack if Donnacona was on
a French ship. Cartier decided to kidnap Taignoagny
and Domagaya as well so they could not spread their
hatred of the French.

Cartier had other reasons for wanting to take
Donnacona back to France. He had almost nothing
to show for his year in Canada, and he had lost
twenty-five men. Because of the many deaths, he was
leaving one ship, the *Petite Hermine,* behind. He had
little gold and only vague hopes of finding a fast trade
route to China. Donnacona would be a prize, of
sorts. The old chief spoke persuasively of having been
to Saguenay and having seen stacks of treasure as well
as white men dressed in wool.

On May 3, 1536, Cartier and his men erected
their second huge cross in the New World, this one
formally claiming Canada for King Francis I. The
next day Donnacona, his sons, and several others
were invited to visit Cartier inside the French
stockade. Donnacona declined. He had been tricked
before and, as a result, had lost his two sons for an
entire year.

Through the interpreters, Donnacona asked
Cartier to take one of his rivals, Agona, back to
France. Cartier lied. He said this was impossible as

*The cross raised by
Cartier at Stadacona.*

the king had instructed him to bring back no native
prisoners. Donnacona believed him and decided to
accept the invitation.

As soon as Donnacona, Taignoagny,
Domagaya, and the others entered the stockade, they
were taken prisoner. Some of those who had come
with Donnacona were allowed to escape. Cartier's

men, muskets at the ready, waited for an attack. The Iroquois gathered outside the stockade and made a great deal of noise. The small fort was surrounded, and fires were lit. All night long the shouting and calling continued, but there was no attack.

By morning the noise had increased, and many warriors had arrived from other villages. Donnacona was escorted onto the deck of the *Grande Hermine* in an attempt to quiet them. He told his people not to worry, he was going to France but would return with a large gift from the French king.

Amazingly, the Iroquois received this news with joy. They presented Cartier with twenty-four strings of esnoguy, necklaces made of shells and trinkets which, as Cartier wrote, "is the greatest wealth they have in this world." Provisions of corn, meat, and fish were brought so Donnacona might eat like a true Iroquois chief during the long voyage.

Cartier and his crew eased their two remaining ships into the river on the morning of May 6. There were ten Iroquois, including Donnacona, Taignoagny, Domagaya and four young children on board. None would return to Canada again.

Cartier also carried a small number of gold nuggets, some of which had been carved into the shape of tiny goose feathers. These nuggets were Cartier's only solid proof that the elusive Kingdom of Saguenay might exist.

The two French ships reached the open sea and sailed past the southern tip of Newfoundland, proving that it was indeed an island. Two months later, on July 6, the expedition sailed back into the harbour of St. Malo.

The Third Voyage

The Grande Hermine.

King Francis I was involved in yet another war and had little immediate interest in the New World. Since he was short of money because of this war, he had even less interest in paying Cartier.

When the war ended early the following year, Cartier was given the *Grande Hermine* as payment for his personal costs in mounting the expedition. The next year he received a cash payment to help with the upkeep of the Iroquois he had brought back with him. Cartier became a coastal trader but spent much of his spare time planning his return to Canada.

Francis I wanted to send another expedition, and

on October 17, 1540, he appointed Cartier as
Captain-General of a new, ambitious expedition,
which was to include tradesmen capable of
establishing a permanent colony in the New World.
At least one priest would also accompany the
explorers. Then, in January, 1541, there was a change
in plans. Francis I decided the colony should be
headed by a "gentleman of the court," Jean-Francois
de La Rocque, known as Roberval. Cartier was
crushed.

*Another
representation of
Cartier.*

Roberval, a nobleman with extensive military
experience, had devised an elaborate plan for the
settlement of Canada. Francis I was convinced the
plan was a good one. Roberval would be given the
powers of a Lord and would pay Francis I one-third
of all profits derived from New World activities.
Roberval would keep one-third of the profits for
himself. The remaining third would be given to minor
noblemen accompanying the expedition. The
noblemen would also receive large sections of land.

Cartier was appointed second-in-command and
put in charge of the fleet. Although he was hurt by
the move, he was still enthusiastic. At least an
expedition was going back to Canada.

Using some of the money he had earned as a
trader, Cartier began to buy his ships. Five large
vessels would be needed to transport the colonists
along with the cows, bulls, sheep, goats, hogs, and
horses they planned to take. When the fleet was
gathered together, more than 250 large animals were
packed on board the ships, the first domestic animals
north of Florida.

Roberval had no problems recruiting noblemen

for the voyage. They, after all, were being promised property and an income. He did have problems recruiting tradesmen, soldiers, and workers. The King finally gave Roberval permission to recruit convicts, although not those found guilty of serious crimes. Prisoners who agreed to go had all their confiscated belongings returned, except for land. They had to pay the cost of their transportation to the New World and food bills for their first two years in the colony. If they should ever return to France without the King's permission they would be condemned without mercy.

Cartier was not happy with the idea of using convicts. He knew the hardships to be faced and he knew how much the colonists would have to rely on each other.

In early May Roberval came to St. Malo to view Cartier's preparations. As a military man, he was not satisfied with the number of artillery pieces or soldiers. He wanted more time to collect a larger army. Cartier reminded Roberval of the King's insistence upon a spring departure. The two men argued and then agreed that Cartier should leave as soon as possible. Roberval would follow. Cartier thought Roberval would leave France a few weeks later, but the two leaders would not meet again for more than a year.

Cartier and his five ships left St. Malo on May 23, 1541. Donnacona and most of the other Iroquois Cartier had brought to France had died. Only one young girl still survived, and Cartier left her behind. Thus, the French still had no interpreter with them.

It was a terrible crossing. The livestock became

Navigation

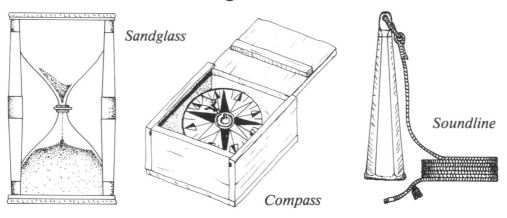

Sandglass

Compass

Soundline

Until the late fifteenth century most navigation was done near land. The main navigational tools were handwritten manuals, usually passed along by a teacher, which told of landmarks, tidal patterns, distances, shoals and safe harbours.

As a young navigator, Jacques Cartier learned to stay on course using a compass and the positions of the stars (useless on a stormy night). The positions of the stars were commonly marked on peg board or paper by the sailor in charge of each watch. The compasses on Cartier's ships would have been kept in large wooden boxes, the bottom painted in a thirty-two point wind rose. In stormy weather such compasses were virtually useless.

Navigators also used a soundline, a lengthy coil of rope, regularly marked with knots, with a lead weight at the end. The weight would be tossed overboard and the depth measured by means of the knots.

Navigators used sandglasses to help determine speed. Often, the best method for finding out how fast a ship was travelling was simply to throw a scrap of wood over the side and time with a sandglass how quickly the vessel sailed away from it.

Cartier also used such simple observation techniques as the colour of the water, the amount of floating debris, and a knowledge of how far certain types of birds fly from shore.

From his journals we know that Cartier was a cautious, careful sailor.

ill. The supply of fresh water ran out, and the animals had to drink cider instead. The ships were scattered but eventually gathered together at Newfoundland. Finally, on August 23, the fleet reached Stadacona.

Agona was now chief. After the natives greeted the ships at the shore, Cartier told them Donnacona had chosen not to return but to live peacefully on his land in France. Donnacona wanted Agona to remain Chief of all Canada. Agona was extremely happy as he now had no rival.

Cartier did not settle into the old stockade site. Instead, he moved upriver to Charlesbourg Royal and quickly had his men build two substantial forts. One fort was at the base of the bluff, next to the ships, and the other was on top of the bluff. Cartier wrote that the land was "as good a country to plow and manure as a man should find or desire."

As they were constructing the fortifications, Cartier's men made what they thought was a remarkable discovery. Hundreds of diamonds and tons of gold lay on the ground simply waiting to be picked up. Cartier and his men did not realize their "gold" was only iron pyrites, or fool's gold, and the "diamonds" were only quartz. The treasure they so enthusiastically collected and protected was worthless.

Cartier's men, an odd assortment of sailors and convicts, were difficult to control. Nobody wanted to make preparations for the winter ahead. Everyone wanted to gather gold and diamonds for himself.

In early September Cartier sent two ships back to France, to inform the King that the expedition had in fact arrived, and that a colony was being established.

In early fall Cartier took two longboats and sailed upriver towards Hochelaga. He did not stay long in the village since he began to detect a change in the Iroquois' attitude towards him. The Iroquois at Hochelaga had heard about the large French gardens and forts and realized that Cartier intended to stay. The Iroquois prized their land above almost anything and often fought other tribes who wanted to live there.

Because of this hostility, Cartier decided not to travel any farther up river. Besides, he thought he had already found mountains of treasure.

Cartier did not keep a full journal during the winter of 1541-42. We know there were cases of scurvy, quickly cured with the help of the white cedar. There is evidence, as well, of a continuing feud with the Iroquois and of grumbling over the gold and diamonds.

The colony survived the winter but found it impossible to plant new crops in the spring. The Iroquois were preparing for a fight. With no sign of Roberval and his soldiers, Cartier decided the King would best be served if he abandoned the colony and returned to France. The ''treasure'' needed to be sent, and Cartier did not trust anyone else to escort it safely.

In May, Cartier and his fleet sailed away from Charlesbourg Royal. The colonists travelled down the St. Lawrence, across to the harbour at St. John's, Newfoundland. Although Cartier did not know it, his commander-in-chief, Roberval, was also at St. John's. A year late, Roberval had finally gathered his army and come to join the colony.

The title page of the English translation of Cartier's first voyage in 1534, published in 1580.

Home to Stay

*The account of Cartier's
second voyage, 1535-36,
published in 1545.*

Roberval and Cartier, with their two fleets of ships, were not the only Europeans in St. John's harbour. There were seventeen other vessels, fishing ships from England, France, and Portugal. It was quite a crowd.

Roberval had been arguing with the Portuguese fishermen over his right to set up a colony in the New World when he saw Cartier arrive. He was shocked. He thought Cartier was more than a thousand kilometres away, settled near Stadacona. Cartier was equally shocked to see Roberval. He had lost hope of ever seeing his commander-in-chief.

The two leaders began to argue as soon as they saw each other. Roberval, the soldier, accused Cartier of having abandoned his post. Cartier replied that the Iroquois were hostile and he had no protection.

Roberval then ordered Cartier to return to the colony with him. Cartier refused, claiming his men were tired and broken in spirit. He also wanted to escort the gold (which was given to an expert at St. John's and reported to be of good quality) back to France.

Cartier and his crew slipped away in the middle of the night, anxious to return to France so that they might present their treasure to King Francis I. Cartier knew the King would forgive his leaving the New World since he brought such riches.

They sailed into the harbour of St. Malo in September, 1542, much to the surprise of the townsfolk, who had not expected Cartier to return for at least another year. Cartier announced that he had found gold and diamonds. Barrel after barrel of treasure was unloaded from the ships to the accompaniment of cheers from those watching.

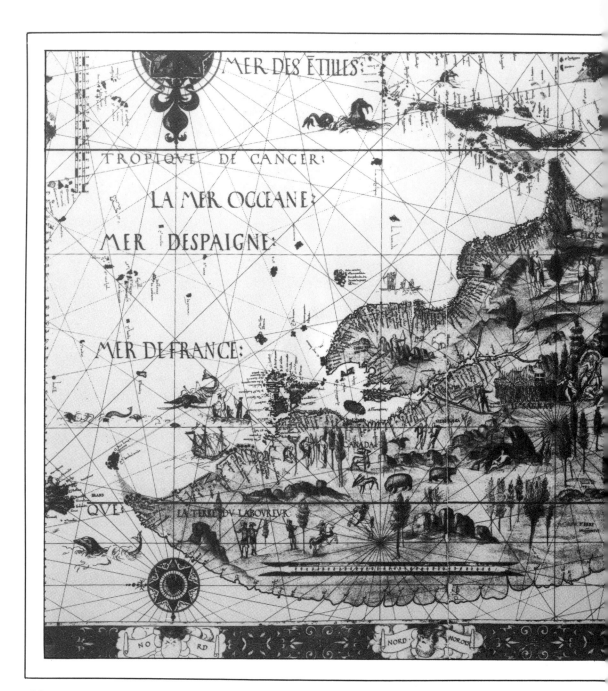

MER·DES·ETILLES·

TROPIQVE· DE· CANCER·

LA·MER·OCCEANE·

MER·DESPAIGNE·

MER·DE·FRANCE·

QVE·

LA·TERRE·DV·LABOVREVR·

After Cartier returned to France, Roberval and his three ships sailed up the St. Lawrence to Stadacona. They reconstructed Cartier's forts, extending them even more. By the time winter arrived, Roberval had built the New World version of a French castle. It had two Great Halls, one for nobility and one for the commoners.

It appears that neither Roberval nor anyone with him knew about the Iroquois cure for scurvy. Fifty colonists died during the harsh winter.

The Iroquois traded peacefully with Roberval. His pilot, Alfonse, called them "good and gentle folk, so that they do no harm to anyone who does none to them."

After wintering in Canada, Roberval decided there was no profit to be made and it was useless to establish a colony there. He made one brief attempt to locate Saguenay and then returned to France.

Roberval gained a reputation as a cruel leader, and many stories arose about his treatment of colonists. He may even have abandoned his daughter on an island in the St. Lawrence after she fell in love with a common soldier.

A map produced by Pierre Descelliers in 1546. Because the map works from south at the top to north at the bottom, the territory it depicts looks more familiar to us if the map is turned upside down. This is one of the first maps to record Cartier's geographical discoveries in the New World. Roberval and his party are depicted above the part of the map marked "Le Sagnay."

Cartier believed he had returned with a fortune.

He had not. A more knowledgeable expert at St. Malo told Cartier that his gold was almost worthless and the diamonds had even less value. Cartier did not believe him and had the treasure checked again and again, with the same result. It was worthless.

Cartier was crushed. "False as a Canadian diamond" became a common term used to describe anything phony or cheap. Some even accused Cartier of mutiny since he had left Roberval when instructed to stay. The King refused to see him, waiting for Roberval to report so he could hear both sides of the story at the same time.

Roberval returned from Canada a year later, after his own attempt to establish a colony had failed. Both men were then summoned before the King so that they might account for their failure. Francis listened to them argue. Although the colony had cost him a great deal of money and effort, the King held neither of the explorers responsible and allowed them to go free.

Jacques Cartier, the only true French explorer of the sixteenth century, retired to a fine stone house near St. Malo, where he lived with his wife, Catherine. He became a respected and active man in the community.

Cartier's accomplishments were remarkable. Through his journals, he provided an articulate, careful record of the beginnings of Canada.

Cartier died at five o'clock in the morning on September 1, 1557. His wife, Catherine, lived alone in their home for many more years.

Cartier's home near St. Malo.

For Discovery

1. Draw a map showing the route of the fishing fleet from St. Malo to Newfoundland. What is the distance (in kilometres) the boats must have sailed?

2. Make a compass similar to the ones the fishermen used. Using it, along with a modern compass, experiment to discover how accurately it gives direction. What do your experiments tell you about the character of the St. Malo fishermen?

3. What would you consider *essential* supplies for a voyage such as Cartier's? Make a list of everything you would want to take with you. How many of the items on your list would have been available to Cartier in 1534?

4. Why do you think there were problems between the Iroquois and Cartier and his men? List as many reasons as you can. Could any of the problems have been avoided? If so, how?

5. What was the biggest problem Cartier faced during his first winter in Canada? Do you think he handled this problem well? What else could he have done?

6. Imagine you are Cartier and write the entry you might make in your diary when you heard that Roberval was to command the third expedition.

7. With a partner act out the conversation between Cartier and the expert who told him the treasure was worthless.

8. In your opinion, what was Cartier's most important contribution to Canada?

Glossary

Cargo A load of goods in transport.

Colonist A citizen of one country who settles in a new land.

Colony A settlement established by citizens of one country in a new land.

Convoys A number of ships travelling together.

Expedition Journey made with a definite purpose.

Longboat A large, strong boat carried by a merchant sailing ship.

Musket A large handgun used before the introduction of the rifle.

Stockade An enclosure made from upright logs used as a defensive fortification.

Index